ACTION FIGURE!

Recent Doonesbury Books by G.B. Trudeau

Read My Lips, Make My Day, Eat Quiche and Die!
Give Those Nymphs Some Hooters!
You're Smokin' Now, Mr. Butts!
I'd Go With the Helmet, Ray
Welcome to Club Scud!
What Is It, Tink, Is Pan in Trouble?
Quality Time on Highway 1
Washed Out Bridges and Other Disasters
In Search of Cigarette Holder Man
Doonesbury Nation
Virtual Doonesbury
Planet Doonesbury
Buck Wild Doonesbury
Duke 2000: Whatever It Takes

Special Collections

The Doonesbury Chronicles
Doonesbury's Greatest Hits
The People's Doonesbury
Doonesbury Dossier: The Reagan Years
Doonesbury Deluxe: Selected Glances Askance
Recycled Doonesbury: Second Thoughts on a Gilded Age
The Portable Doonesbury
Flashbacks: Twenty-Five Years of Doonesbury
The Bundled Doonesbury

ACTION FIGURE!

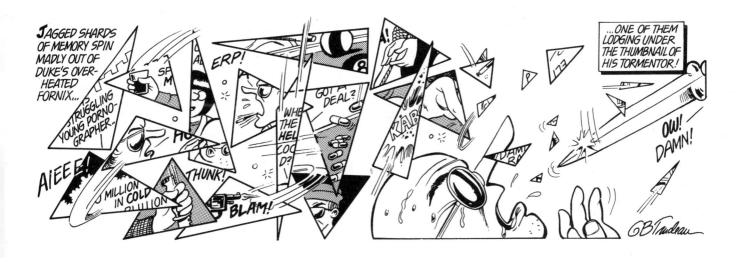

**Andrews McMeel
Publishing**

Kansas City

00 01 02 03 04 BAH 10 9 8 7 6 5 4 3 2 1

ISBN: 0-7407-1554-2

Library of Congress Catalog Card Number: 00-109126

Doonesbury may be viewed on the Internet at:
www.doonesbury.com and www.uexpress.com

── **ATTENTION: SCHOOLS AND BUSINESSES** ──

Andrews McMeel books are available at quantity discounts with bulk purchase for educational, business, or sales promotional use. For information, please write to: Special Sales Department, Andrews McMeel Publishing, 4520 Main Street, Kansas City, Missouri 64111.

"Just waking up in the morning
means a lot to me."
— Keith Richards

18

23

LOOK, BOY WONDER, YOU **CAN'T** TAKE ME OFF THE MASTHEAD!—MY READERS WILL HAVE YOUR **HEAD**!

WHAT READERS?! YOU HAVEN'T PRODUCED AN ARTICLE IN **YEARS**!

DUKE, IF YOU WANT TO STAY WITH THIS ORGANIZATION, YOU'RE GOING TO HAVE TO START PAYING SOME DUES AGAIN! I'M REASSIGNING YOU TO THE ROCK 'N' ROLL BEAT!

ROCK 'N' ROLL BEAT?! ARE YOU **MAD**!

YOUR FIRST PROJECT WILL BE AN UPDATE REPORT ON CHER.

A WRITER OF MY STATURE?!

CHER'S COOL— SHE WON'T MIND.

YOU'RE QUITE MAD, YOU KNOW. NO **WAY** I'M GOING TO COVER CHER!

YES, YOU ARE, DUKE! OR YOU DISAPPEAR FROM THE MASTHEAD FOR GOOD!

YOU **PUP**! YOU CAN'T **DO** THIS TO ME!

WHY? WHERE YOU GOING TO GO, DUKE— "LADIES HOME JOURNAL"?

DO YOU HAVE **ANY** IDEA WHAT EVEN A **TEMPORARY** GREGG AND CHER GIG COULD DO TO MY REP?

TEMPORARY? WHO SAID ANYTHING ABOUT TEMPORARY? I'M MAKING YOU BUREAU CHIEF!

GREGG AND CHER BUREAU CHIEF?!

AND I'M ONLY DOING IT BECAUSE WE'RE OLD FRIENDS.

WELL, DUKE, I'M SURE YOU'RE ANXIOUS TO MEET THE REST OF OUR CHER TASK FORCE!

CHER **WHAT**?!

MICHELLE HERE IS IN CHARGE OF THE MOBILE SURVEILLANCE UNITS... AND THAT'S ANNIE, WHO'S AN EXPERT ON CHER'S MEN. SHE ALSO CO-ORDINATES PAPARAZZI ACTIVITIES.

HI.

LESTER OVER THERE IS OUR INSIDE MAN..

INSIDE MAN?

YEAH— I'M A CLOSE PERSONAL FRIEND OF CHER'S DERMATOLOGIST.

WELL, I'M SURE YOU'VE GOT A LOT TO TALK ABOUT!

I'LL GET YOU FOR THIS..

WE GREW UP TOGETHER!

34

AS FAR AS DETENTE IS CONCERNED, WE'LL JUST HAVE TO SEE WHAT DEVELOPS. I'M SURE MY CHINESE HOSTS WOULD BE AS SADDENED TO SEE U.S. GUNBOATS STEAMING UP THE YANGTZE AS I WOULD BE.

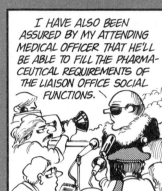

SIR, DO YOU EXPECT TO CONTINUE INGESTING RECREATIONAL DRUGS DURING YOUR STAY IN CHINA?

ABSOLUTELY— I INTEND TO STRESS CONTINUITY IN MY PERSONAL HABITS!

I HAVE ALSO BEEN ASSURED BY MY ATTENDING MEDICAL OFFICER THAT HE'LL BE ABLE TO FILL THE PHARMACEUTICAL REQUIREMENTS OF THE LIAISON OFFICE SOCIAL FUNCTIONS.

BUT, SIR, AS YOU MUST KNOW, YOUR CHINESE HOSTS FROWN ON ALL FORMS OF EXCESS.

MY CHINESE HOSTS CAN GO SUCK EGGS.

A LIGHT DRIZZLE GREETED THE NEW CHIEF OF THE U.S. MISSION AS HIS PLANE TOUCHED DOWN HERE AT PEKING INTERNATIONAL AIRPORT..

THE PASSENGER DOOR OF THE AIRCRAFT HAS BEEN OPENED, AND CHINESE OFFICIALS ARE NOW GATHERING ON THE RUNWAY TO MEET THE NEW TOP ENVOY.

THE GREETING IS EXPECTED TO BE STRAINED, AS AMBASSADOR DUKE IS KNOWN TO BE OPENLY SUSPICIOUS OF HIS CHINESE HOSTS.

COVER ME— I THINK I CAN MAKE THE LIMO!

BUT, SIR— IT'S ONLY AN HONOR GUARD..

A FURTHER GOAL OF MINE IS THE SPEEDY IMPLEMENTATION OF NORMALIZATION.

(A FURTHER GOAL OF HIS IS THE SPEEDY IMPLEMENTATION OF NORMALIZATION.)

LASTLY, I COME TO CHINA IN THE HOPE OF FULFILLING A LIFE-LONG AMBITION — DROPPING ACID ON THE GREAT WALL.

(LASTLY, HE WISHES YOU GOOD HEALTH AND LONG LIFE.)

IN CONCLUSION, LET ME JUST SAY THAT I LOOK FORWARD TO A NEW SPIRIT OF CO-OPERATION FROM OUR CHINESE FRIENDS. I SINCERELY HOPE IT WON'T BE NECESSARY TO SHELL ANY PAGODAS.

(HE ALSO WISHES YOUR WIFE GOOD HEALTH.)

(THANK HIM, AND ASK HIM IF HE'D LIKE TO SEE THE GREAT WALL.)

"..AND BECAUSE MY CHINESE HOSTS WERE SO EAGER TO ORIENT ME, ENDLESS SIGHTSEEING BECAME MY MAJOR ACTIVITY."

"UNFORTUNATELY, THE GREATEST SIGHT OF ALL, THE CHAIRMAN HIMSELF, ELUDED ME FOR A SOLID MONTH. I BEGAN TO WONDER IF HE'D EVER SURFACE."

"THEN FINALLY LAST WEDNESDAY, AT 3:30 A.M., THE CALL CAME.."

HURRY, SIR— NO TIME TO WASTE!

ALRIGHT, ALRIGHT— JUST LET ME PUT MY PANTS ON, OKAY?!

TELL ME, HONEY— IS IT HARD TO CONVERSE WITH THE CHAIRMAN? I WAS TOLD HIS STROKE LEFT HIM WITH A SPEECH IMPAIRMENT..

YES, SIR. CHAIRMAN MAO HAS ALWAYS BEEN HARD TO UNDERSTAND BECAUSE HE SPEAKS AN OBSCURE RURAL DIALECT. AND NOW WITH THE STROKE, I SEEM TO BE THE ONLY TRANSLATOR WHO CAN STILL UNDERSTAND HIM.

NO KIDDING?.. MAN, THAT CERTAINLY LEAVES YOU WITH A HELL OF A RESPONSIBILITY, DOESN'T IT?

YES, SIR. IN A WAY, I'M SORT OF RUNNING THE COUNTRY.

I'LL KEEP THAT IN MIND.

..AND I BRING HIM GREETINGS FROM THE AMERICAN PEOPLE.

(AND HE BRINGS YOU GREETINGS FROM THE AMERICAN PEOPLE.)

(MMPHPH SPMUP LI MXZPQU!)

WHAT'D HE SAY?

THE CHAIRMAN SAYS IT GIVES HIM GREAT PLEASURE TO SEE HIS OLD FRIEND DAVID EISENHOWER AGAIN.

YOU MADE THAT UP, RIGHT? THINKING IT FUNNY?

I CALL THEM AS I HEAR THEM, SIR.

47

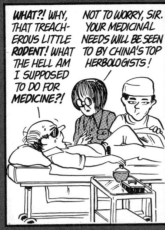

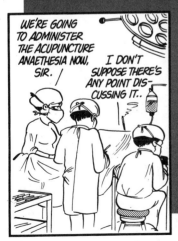

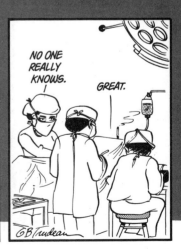

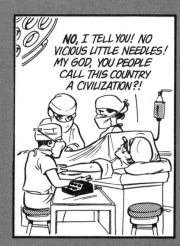

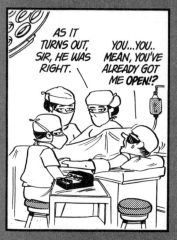

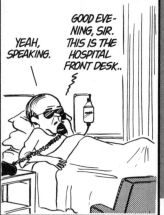

MR. DUKE, HAVE YOU STARTED YOUR SPEECH FOR TONIGHT'S BANQUET YET?

YEAH, HONEY, I GOT A FEW IDEAS DOWN. I'LL PROBABLY JUST WING IT, THOUGH.

IS THAT WISE, SIR? THE WHOLE CENTRAL COMMITTEE WILL BE IN ATTENDANCE.

LOOK, DON'T WORRY! IT'S JUST ANOTHER BANQUET GIG, HONEY!

I MEAN, I ACED THAT UNIVERSITY BANQUET DIDN'T I? YOU KNOW, WITH MY ADDRESS ON AMERICAN HUMOR?

I THOUGHT THOSE WERE POLISH JOKES, SIR.

YEAH, BUT THEY ORIGINATED IN THE STATES!

..AND I THANK MY CHINESE HOSTS FOR THEIR RELENTLESS HOSPITALITY!

(HE THANKS YOU FOR BEING HOSPITABLE.)

THE LAST YEAR HAS PASSED WITHOUT ANY MAJOR PROVOCATION AND I APPRECIATE THAT.

(HE THANKS YOU FOR BEING SO TOLERANT.)

I LOOK FORWARD TO MANY MORE YEARS OF WORKING WITH PEKING!

(HE DOESN'T KNOW YET HE'S BEING REPLACED BY LEONARD WOODCOCK.)

YOU'RE NOT PROJECTING, HONEY.

(HE DOESN'T KNOW YET HE'S BEING REPLACED BY LEONARD WOODCOCK!)

THERE'S BEEN A LOT OF TALK LATELY THAT JIMMY CARTER HAS BEEN IGNORING CHINA!

(HE BRINGS YOU GREETINGS FROM PRESIDENT CARTER!)

WELL, THERE'S A REASON FOR THAT! THE HUMAN RIGHTS SITUATION HERE IS SO BAD IT BOGGLES THE MIND!

(HE BRINGS GREETINGS FROM VICE-PRESIDENT MONDALE!)

CLAP! CLAP! CLAP! CLAP! CLAP! CLAP! CLAP!

WHY ARE THEY APPLAUDING, HONEY?

THEY LOVE YOU, SIR.

..AND ART BUCHWALD'S NOT AVAILABLE EITHER, WHICH MEANS WE'VE GOT ONLY ONE WEEK LEFT TO FIND SOMEONE TO GIVE THIS YEAR'S JOURNALISM LECTURE!

ABE, I'VE GOT A SUGGESTION! HOW ABOUT FORMER AMBASSADOR DUKE, THE EX-GONZO STRINGER FOR "ROLLING STONE"?

HIS IS A UNIQUE PERSPECTIVE ON THE DARK UNDERSIDE OF OUTLAW JOURNALISM. AND HIS IMMENSE POPULARITY AMONG US KIDS WOULD LEND A CACHET TO THE LECTURE!

ACCORDING TO WHOM?

ZONKER. I'VE NEVER HEARD OF HIM MYSELF.

TRUST ME, GUYS. HE'D BE PERFECT! REALLY!

GOOD LORD, KID, IT'S ONLY SEVEN O'CLOCK! HAVEN'T YOU EVER HEARD OF TIME ZONES?

YES, SIR, I'M SORRY, SIR, BUT WE'RE KIND OF PRESSED. YOUR NEPHEW SAID IT WOULD BE OKAY TO CALL..

MY NEPHEW? ZONKER?

YES, SIR. HE'S ON THE SPEAKER'S COMMITTEE WITH ME..

LOOK, CHIEF, I DON'T GIVE A DAMN IF HE'S ON THE SAME..

AND HE SAID TO BE SURE TO MENTION THE $3,000. HONORARIUM TO YOU!

THAT RASCAL. HE REALLY SAID THAT?

YES, SIR. HE SEEMS TO THINK THE WORLD OF YOU.

MR. DUKE! MR. DUKE! OVER HERE, SIR!

HELLO?

I'M RONNIE, SIR! DID YOU HAVE A GOOD FLIGHT?

YEAH, IT WAS OKAY.

LET ME JUST SAY, SIR, HOW VERY HONORED WE ALL ARE THAT YOU WERE ABLE TO TAKE TIME FROM YOUR BUSY SCHEDULE TO COME SPEAK TO US!

UH-HUH. GOT MY FEE WITH YOU?

OH, YES, OF COURSE, SIR. IN TENS AND TWENTIES, AS REQUESTED.

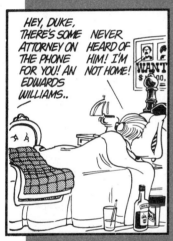

GOOD NEWS, UNCLE DUKE?

YOU BET IT IS, NEPHEW! OL' MAN WILLIAMS WANTS TO INTERVIEW ME FOR THE REDSKINS MANAGER POSITION!

YOU? HOW COME?

WELL, HE CHECKED OUT MY RESUME AND CLIPPINGS FROM MY SPORTS WRITING DAYS..

AMONG OTHER THINGS, IT SEEMS HE WAS QUITE IMPRESSED WITH MY DETAILED KNOWLEDGE OF THE NEW WORK THAT'S BEING DONE WITH HIGH-PERFORMANCE STEROIDS!

A MANAGER NEEDS TO KNOW THAT?

OH, ABSOLUTELY! WHY DO YOU THINK HE HAD TO LET GEORGE ALLEN GO?

MR. DUKE, I THINK YOU'RE QUITE MISTAKEN ABOUT THE EXTENT OF THE PILL PROBLEM. WHY, NFL OFFICIALS GIVE ANTI-DRUG LECTURES EVERY MONTH..

YEAH, AND 90% OF YOUR PLAYERS ARE LAUGHING THEIR JOCKS OFF THE WHOLE TIME!

MR. WILLIAMS, YOUR PLAYERS AREN'T PILLHEADS BECAUSE THEY **WANT** TO BE. HELL, NOBODY **LIKES** TAKING PILLS! THEY TAKE 'EM BECAUSE THEY'RE CONCERNED ABOUT WHAT THE NEXT ATHLETE MIGHT BE DOING!

OH.. OH, I SEE.

IT'S A REAL PROBLEM, SIR! AND I'LL TELL YOU, SOMETIMES IT JUST BREAKS MY HEART TO SEE IT!

BUT YOU SAY YOU'VE HAD SOME EXPERIENCE IN THIS AREA?

I'VE BEEN AROUND THE TRACK A FEW TIMES, YES.

MR. WILLIAMS, I HOPE I'M NOT BEING OUT OF LINE IN TELLING YOU THAT I THINK I UNDERSTAND YOUR PROBLEM. BASICALLY, YOU'RE HOT FOR THE SUPER BOWL!

CAN YOU GET ME THERE, MR. DUKE?

WITH TIME? WITHOUT QUESTION, SIR! BUT I'D BE REMISS IF I FAILED TO MENTION THAT MY TALENTS ARE IN CONSIDERABLE DEMAND NOW!

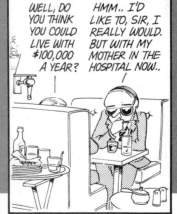

WELL, DO YOU THINK YOU COULD LIVE WITH $100,000 A YEAR?

HMM.. I'D LIKE TO, SIR, I REALLY WOULD. BUT WITH MY MOTHER IN THE HOSPITAL NOW..

PITY. COULD YOU SUGGEST ANYONE ELSE WHO..

OH, THE HECK WITH MOM! THIS IS TOO IMPORTANT!

77

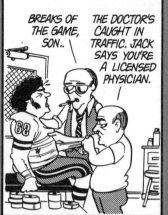

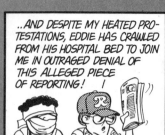

82

WELL! THE STUDENTS CERTAINLY SEEM TO BE FASCINATED BY YOUR MR. DUKE!

UH-HUH. SAY, WHO'S THE YOUNG LADY WHO HAS BEEN MONOPOLIZING HIM?

THAT'S MS. HUAN. SHE'S FROM PEKING.

ACCORDING TO HER, SHE AND MR. DUKE WERE CLOSE FRIENDS DURING HIS TOUR OF DUTY IN CHINA..

WILL YOU BE SHOWING ME WASHINGTON BY NIGHT, SIR?

CAN'T MAKE ANY SUDDEN MOVES.. HAVE TO STAY CALM..

EXCUSE ME, SIRS. I WONDER IF YOU COULD TELL ME WHERE I MIGHT FIND MR. DUKE..

SHOULD BE IN THE CLUBHOUSE, MISS. FIRST DOOR ON THE RIGHT.

THANK YOU.

NOT AT ALL.

MAY I JUST SAY YOU'RE QUITE A PAIR OF SPECIMENS, SIRS.

PART OF THE JOB, MISS.

YOU SHOULD SEE THE GUYS WHO START.

THERE YOU ARE, SIR!

OH, NO..

I'VE BEEN LOOKING ALL OVER FOR YOU! I'VE JUST BEEN TALKING TO YOUR RESERVE QUARTERBACK! WHAT A GREAT GUY!

THIS BETTER BE AN AFTER-EFFECT..

LISTEN, I THINK YOU SHOULD PLAY HIM. HE'S MUCH BETTER LOOKING THAN THE GUY YOU GOT PLAYING NOW.

USED TO BE A TIME WHEN YOU KNEW WHAT WENT INTO THIS STUFF..

UM.. YOU'RE NOT GOING TO CHANGE FOR OUR DATE, SIR?

THAT DOES IT! I'M SWITCHING PHARMACISTS!

86

"MOTHER"! A CABLE FROM TEHERAN!

FINALLY! GIVE IT HERE!

"REGRET TO IN-FORM YOU EAGLE HAS BOMBED. DIPSTICK."

MOTHER OF ALLAH! THEY CAUGHT HIM ALREADY?

GOD HELP US ALL.

A TOURIST? WITH OVER $200,000 IN CASH?

SO I'M NOT KARL MALDEN. SUE ME.

GOOD EVENING. TODAY FORMER UNITED STATES AMBASSADOR DUKE WAS CAPTURED WHILE PARA-CHUTING INTO THE AHVAZ OIL FIELDS IN IRAN. ROLAND HEDLEY HAS DETAILS.

THE REVOLUTIONARY GOVERNMENT OF THE AYATOLLAH KHOMEINI ANNOUNCED TONIGHT THAT THE ONETIME WASHINGTON REDSKINS FIELD GENERAL WOULD BE TRIED AND CONVICTED OF HIGH CRIMES AGAINST GOD.

ALTHOUGH DUE PROCESS AS PRACTICED IN THE WEST IS VIRTUALLY UNKNOWN HERE, ABC NEWS HAS LEARNED THAT AMBASSA-DOR DUKE WAS PERMITTED THE CUSTOMARY PHONE CALL..

HEY, MAN, THOSE ARE THE BREAKS.

DAMMIT, BRENNER! I NEED THOSE KRUGGERRANDS!

THIS IS ROLAND HEDLEY. IT'S A BLEAK, DARK MORNING HERE IN TEHERAN AS THE ESPIONAGE TRIAL OF FORMER AMBASSADOR DUKE GETS UNDER WAY!

IN THE NEW IRAN, THE ISLAMIC KANGAROO COURTS ARE CUSTOM-ARILY GAVELED TO ORDER AT AN UNGODLY 4:00 A.M.! TODAY SHOULD BE NO EXCEPTION.

TENSION HAS BEEN MOUNTING HERE ALL WEEK AS..

THE WHOLE WORLD IS WATCHING! THE WHOLE WORLD IS WATCHING!

AH, HERE COMES THE DEFENDANT NOW!

THE WHOLE.. >THUD!< UNH!

MR. DUKE WAS THEN DRAGGED SCREAMING AND KICKING TO THE GRAVEL ROOFTOP OF THE COURTHOUSE, A POPULAR SPOT IN RECENT MONTHS FOR DISCIPLINING FORMER SAVAK AGENTS.

AS YET, HOWEVER, THERE HAS BEEN NO OFFICIAL INDICATION THAT THE SENTENCE HAS BEEN CARRIED OUT. CERTAINLY THIS REPORTER HAS HEARD NO SHOTS, AND HE HAS KEPT HIS EARS PRICKED.

MOREOVER, THERE ARE NOW REPORTS THAT SENSITIVE NEGOTIATIONS MAY BE UNDER WAY IN A LAST-DITCH ATTEMPT TO SAVE THE FORMER AMBASSADOR'S LIFE.

$500,000! IN GOLD!

$250,000! AND THAT'S MY FINAL OFFER!

WHAT'S IT SAY, ZONK?

"REGRET TO INFORM YOU YOUR UNCLE DUKE HAS BEEN DECLARED LEGALLY DEAD."

"READING OF WILL SCHEDULED FOR MONDAY. PLEASE COME SOONEST TO HELP ORGANIZE PERSONAL EFFECTS. CONDOLENCES. T. BANNON, ATTORNEY-AT-LAW."

GEE.. WHO DO YOU SUPPOSE MOVED TO HAVE HIM DECLARED LEGALLY DEAD?

I'M NOT SURE, BUT I'VE GOT A PRETTY GOOD IDEA!

YOU WANT THE STEREO PACKED TOO, BUDDY?

NO, NO, JUST PUT IT IN THE BACK OF MY VAN.

THIS SIDE UP

FRAGILE

IS THAT YOU, BRENNER?

HEY, ZONK! GOOD TO SEE YOU AGAIN, MAN!

DUKE

BRENNER, WHAT THE HELL IS GOING ON? WHO HAD DUKE DECLARED DEAD?

IT HAD TO BE DONE SOONER OR LATER, MAN. LIFE GOES ON, YOU KNOW?

DUKE

SO YOU WROTE HIM OFF? JUST LIKE THAT?

WELL, WE WERE THINKING OF A MEMORIAL SERVICE, BUT HIS ATTORNEY AND I FIGURED WE OUGHTA TRY TO KEEP EXPENSES DOWN.

DUKE

AS A COURTESY TO HIS HEIRS, NO DOUBT.

RIGHT. BESIDES, I COULDN'T REMEMBER WHICH CULT HE BELONGED TO.

DUKE

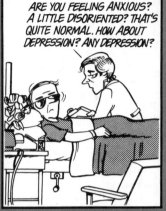

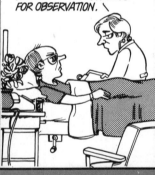

ON THE LAM

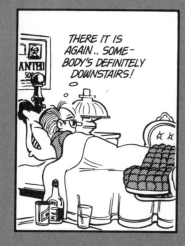

118

ISN'T SHE A BEAUT, HONEY? THE OWNER'S HAVING A FEW LEGAL PROBLEMS RIGHT NOW, SO HE'S WILLING TO LET HER GO FOR ONLY $2,000!

$2,000? WHERE WOULD I GET *THAT* KIND OF MONEY, SIR?

I'M SURE YOU'LL THINK OF SOMETHING. BESIDES, I'D PAY YOU BACK RIGHT AFTER THE FIRST HAUL!

DEEP-SEA CHARTERS PAY THAT WELL, SIR?

THEY DO ON THESE BIG TWIN-ENGINE JOBS! THEY JUST DON'T *BUILD* THEM LIKE THIS ANYMORE, HONEY!

AND YOU SAY SHE'S IN GOOD SHAPE?

PERFECT! WELL, THE DECK GUN MAY NEED A LITTLE WORK..

CYNTHIA? HI, IT'S J.J. LISTEN, IS HONEY OVER THERE AT THE SORORITY BY ANY CHANCE?

NO? GEE, THAT'S STRANGE. I CAN'T SEEM TO FIND HER ANYWHERE..

LOOK, IF SHE COMES IN, WILL YOU TELL HER THAT HER EMBASSY IS TRYING TO REACH HER ABOUT SOME NEW STUDENT LOAN SHE JUST TOOK OUT?

I DECIDED TO FOLLOW MY HEART, SIR.

GREAT. DID YOU BRING THE MONEY?

GIVE!!

AHOY!

SI?

ARE YOU RODRIGUEZ?

SI, AMIGO! YOU MUST BE SENOR DUKE! WHO IS THAT WITH YOU?

MY FAITHFUL ORIENTAL COMPANION. CAN WE COME UP AND SEE THE BOAT?

BY ALL MEANS! YOU ARE MOST WELCOME ABOARD!

EXCUSE ME, SIR. WOULD YOU HAVE SOME PLACE I COULD CHANGE INTO MY BIKINI?

TRY THE CAR, HONEY. THIS IS A BUSINESS MEETING!

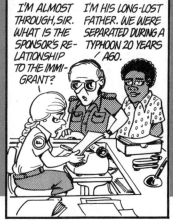

 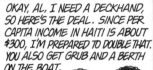

139

143

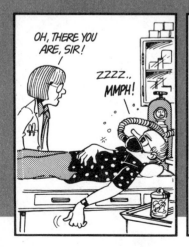

..AND CALL THE LABOR MINISTRY. WE'RE GOING TO NEED SCABS TO SERVE LUNCH AFTER THE CEREMONY.

THAT WON'T BE NECESSARY, SIR. I SETTLED THE KITCHEN WORKER STRIKE LAST NIGHT.

YOU DID? NOW, THAT'S THE BEST NEWS I'VE HAD ALL WEEK! GOOD WORK, HONEY!

THANK YOU, SIR. I WONDER IF YOU'D LIKE TO GO THROUGH THE LIST OF TODAY'S HONORARY DEGREE RECIPIENTS.

SURE, WHY NOT? LET'S SEE.. PAUL LUMIÈRE. JEANNE GENOT. PIERRE BERGER. ADRIENNE D'ARCY. IMPRESSIVE LINE-UP, HONEY!

YES, SIR.

WHO THE HELL ARE THEY?

THE KITCHEN STAFF.

ARE THE STUDENTS ALL LINED UP FOR THE ACADEMIC PROCESSION, DEAN HONEY?

AS MANY AS WE COULD FIND, YES, SIR.

AS MANY AS YOU COULD FIND?

WELL, SIR, THE HURRICANE LAST WEEK CAUSED SOME BIG SWELLS ON THE NORTH SHORE. A LOT OF THE STUDENTS ARE SURFING.

SURFING? THE MORNING OF MY INAUGURATION? DAMMIT, DEAN HONEY, I WILL **NOT** TOLERATE THIS KIND OF DISRESPECT TOWARD THE OFFICE OF THE PRESIDENCY!

I WANT THEM **EXPELLED!** EVERY LAST **MOTHER'S** SON!

YOU CAN'T DO THAT, SIR. YOU PUT THEIR TUITION INTO FIVE-YEAR BONDS.

BEFORE I INTRODUCE THE INAUGURAL SPEAKER, A FEW WORDS. IN THE MONTHS AHEAD, YOU WILL ALL STUDY MEDICINE. YOU WILL PLAY GOLF. YOU WILL LEARN ABOUT TAX SHELTERS. IN SHORT, YOU WILL BECOME DOCTORS!

BUT COME FEBRUARY, LADIES AND GENTLEMEN, YOU WILL DO THE **MOST IMPORTANT** THING YOU'LL **EVER** DO IN YOUR LIVES! YOU WILL MEET ST. GEORGE'S IN GRENADA, AND YOU WILL **DESTROY** THEM IN VOLLEYBALL!

YEAAA!

CLAP! CLAP! CLAP! CLAP!

GRENADA SUCKS EGGS! GRENADA SUCKS EGGS!

POINT SPREAD CITY!

THEY SURE HAVE A LOT OF SCHOOL SPIRIT, SIR.

WITH THAT SIMPLE CHEMICAL RECONFIGURATION, "INTENSITY" CAME KICKING INTO THE WORLD.

WE JUST FIGURED WHY GO WITH TWO OXYGEN MOLECULES WHEN ONE WILL DO?

THE DRUG, BY THE WAY, IS INSANELY GREAT. WE FORESEE MYRIAD APPLICATIONS IN PSYCHIATRY AND PROFESSIONAL FOOTBALL.

ANY SIDE EFFECTS, DR. GORP?

YES, BUT INTRIGUING ONES. FOR EXAMPLE, "INTENSITY" GIVES THE ILLUSION OF SUBSTANCE TO YOUR ALTER EGO.

UH.. HOLD IT, ALBIE. ARE YOU IMPLYING I'M ONLY A SIDE EFFECT?

IT'S ONLY TEMPORARY, THOUGH.

©B Trudeau

DR. GORP, ARE THERE ANY OTHER SIDE EFFECTS ASSOCIATED WITH "INTENSITY" WE SHOULD BE AWARE OF?

WELL, YES, "INTENSITY" SEEMS TO SHARE SOME OF THE MILD UNPLEASANTNESS ATTRIBUTED TO ITS CHEMICAL COUSINS..

.. LIKE NAUSEA, TIGHTENING OF THE JAW, SOME DIZZINESS..

BAD NEWS, ALBIE. TRICKY DICK GOT THE G.O.P. NOMINATION!

.. AND, OF COURSE, FLASHBACKS.

DR. GORP, HAVE YOU WORKED OUT THE ETHICAL RAMIFICATIONS OF MARKETING A DESIGNER DRUG AS UNTESTED AS "INTENSITY"?

NO, BUT MY TWIN BROTHER BUNNY HAS, RIGHT, BUNNY?

THAT'S RIGHT, ALBIE..

I'VE DONE A LOT OF RESEARCH ON THE MATTER, AND I CAN ASSURE YOU, MORALS-WISE, WE'RE ON TERRA FIRMA.

SIR, IF YOU HIRE THE SIDE EFFECT, I'M QUITTING.

NOW, DEAN HONEY, I CAN'T BREAK UP THE ACT.

©B Trudeau

SIR! WAKE UP! YOU'RE MISSING ALL THE EXCITEMENT!

WHAT?.. >SNORT!< WHAT EXCITEMENT?

ZONKER'S PRESS CONFERENCE ON HIS LOTTERY PRIZE!

HE GOT SO MANY CALLS FROM THE MEDIA THIS WEEKEND, HE DECIDED TO READ A PREPARED STATEMENT ABOUT HIS PLANS.

"..AND, OF COURSE, I'LL BE DATING SHOW GIRLS."

BEFORE THE CHECK CLEARS?

ZONKER! HOW DID YOU FEEL WHEN YOU HEARD THE GOOD NEWS?

YEAH, WHAT WERE YOUR FEELINGS?

COULD YOU DESCRIBE THEM?

WELL, AT FIRST I DIDN'T FEEL ANYTHING. I JUST WENT NUMB.

THEN I FELT A RUSH OF GIDDINESS, FOLLOWED BY FEELINGS OF DIS-ORIENTATION, QUEASINESS, SHORTNESS OF BREATH..

..HUNGER, RAGE, SEXUAL LONGING, VERTIGO, BOREDOM, AND FINALLY, A TINGLING SENSATION.

WHAT ABOUT AFTER THE NEWS SUNK IN?

LADIES AND GENTLEMEN, THE BOTTOM LINE HERE IS THAT NO AMOUNT OF MONEY COULD EVER INTERFERE WITH MY DREAM OF ESTABLISHING A PRIVATE MEDICAL PRACTICE IN SOUTH-ERN CALIFORNIA.

WHAT ABOUT CHARITY, ZONKER?

HOW DOES YOUR FAMILY FEEL?

WHAT'S THE TAX BITE?

HEY, HEY, YOU NETWORK BOYS HAVE BEEN HOG-GING ALL THE QUESTIONS. LET'S LET THE SUPERMARKET MEDIA GET IN A FEW, OKAY?

ZONKER, ABOUT YOUR LOVE-CHILD WITH MRS. GORBACHEV..

ZONKER, WILL YOU BE SLAYING MOM, CO-ED, SELF?

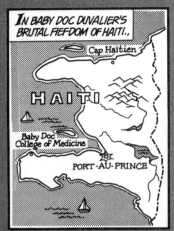

IN BABY DOC DUVALIER'S BRUTAL FIEFDOM OF HAITI..

..WHERE THE SECRET RITES OF VODOUN ARE PRACTICED MUCH AS THEY WERE 200 YEARS AGO..

..A SOUL-SEARING SCREAM PIERCING THE STILL OF THE NIGHT..

AAIEE!

..HARDLY RAISES AN EYEBROW.

KEEP IT DOWN, SIR!

CARRIED ALONG BY GENTLE TRADE WINDS OFF HAITI..

..A SOLITARY FLY..

..BEGINS HIS DAY.

BZZZZZ!

SIR? SIR?

GOOD MORNING, SIR. TIME FOR YOUR VITAMIN PICK-ME-UP!

YOU'RE LOOKING MORE INERT THAN USUAL THIS MORNING, SIR.. HEY, WHERE'S YOUR VEIN?..

HMM.. NO PULSE, EITHER. PALLID COMPLEXION, DILATED PUPILS.. SIR, IF I DIDN'T KNOW YOU BETTER, MEDICALLY SPEAKING, I'D SAY YOU WERE..

..DEAD.

AN OVERDOSE JUST DOESN'T MAKE SENSE, CURTIS. DUKE KNEW HIS LIMITS.

LET'S GO OVER IT AGAIN, DEAN HONEY. WHEN DID YOU LAST SEE HIM?

AROUND 10 P.M. HE'D JUST HAD HIS MASSAGE AND HE WAS UNWINDING WITH A FIFTH OF..

WAIT A MINUTE, A MASSAGE? WHO GAVE HIM THE MASSAGE?

JUST A BURSARY STUDENT FROM THE VOODOO CENTER..

VOODOO? THAT'S IT! DUKE ISN'T DEAD, HE'S A ZOMBIE! WE BURIED HIM ALIVE!

THIS HAS GOT TO BE THE WORST HANGOVER OF MY ENTIRE LIFE..

THE MASSEUSE FROM THE VOODOO CENTER HAS MYSTERIOUSLY DISAPPEARED!

THEN I WAS RIGHT, DEAN HONEY! DUKE HAS BEEN ZOMBIFIED!

HOW EXACTLY IS THAT DONE, SIR?

THE VICTIM IS POISONED TOPICALLY WITH THE TOXIN OF A PUFFER FISH..

IT REDUCES HIS METABOLIC RATE TO THE POINT WHERE HE APPEARS DEAD! HE'S THEN BURIED, AND LATER DUG UP AND REVIVED BY A VOODOO SORCERER..

SOUNDS LIKE SOME CRAZY FRATERNITY STUNT.

..AND THEN SOLD INTO SLAVERY!

ARE YOU SURE ABOUT THIS ZOMBIE STUFF, SIR?

POSITIVE! COME ON, WE'VE GOT TO GET BACK TO THE GRAVEYARD BEFORE THE BOKOR!

THE WHAT?

THE VOODOO SORCERER WHO DID HIM IN! WHO KNOWS WHAT EVIL PURPOSE HE HAS IN STORE FOR DUKE!

I DUNNO, SIR. DUKE WOULD NEVER SUBMIT TO SOME WITCH DOCTOR!

HE WILL AFTER HE'S FED THE BOKOR'S PASTE! IT CRUSHES THE FREE WILL AND SPIRIT OF THE ZOMBIE!

HOW DO YOU KNOW ALL THIS STUFF, SIR?

I'M DATING ONE. THEY'RE REAL EASY TO TALK TO.

THE INTERVIEW'S ON? FANTASTIC!

ANY GROUND RULES? WHAT'S HE PREPARED TO COVER?

UH-HUH.. RETIREMENT, RIGHT.. HIS PLACE IN HISTORY.. UH-HUH.. NO, I DON'T HAVE ANY PROBLEMS WITH THAT.

TIP O'NEILL?

BABY DOC.

LOOK AT THOSE FACES. ARROGANT TO THE END! WOULDN'T YOU **LOVE** TO KNOW WHAT THE DUVALIERS SPIRITED OUT WITH THEM THE NIGHT THEY FLED?

WELL, YES AND NO..

FRIDAY, FEB

Duvalier Lea

he final drive to the airport. AP

"powerful as a monkey's tail." U.S. of- decided to give up his auth.. Baby Doc has

SOMETIMES, THE REAL STORY CAN BE..

..UNSPEAKABLY HIDEOUS!

..AND RICK'S ALREADY LEFT TO VISIT HIM IN EXILE. IT'S ONE OF THE FEW INTERVIEWS DUVALIER'S EVER GIVEN!

GOODNESS! THAT **IS** A REMARKABLE ASSIGNMENT!

IT SHOULD YIELD SOME ABSOLUTELY **FASCINATING** INSIGHTS INTO THE GENESIS OF EVIL!

.. AND THEN THE OTHER KIDS STARTED CALLING ME "BASKETHEAD."

SO THAT'S WHEN YOU DECIDED TO GET EVEN?

MR. DUPUIS? YES, THIS IS MR. HARRIS. I UNDERSTAND YOU REPRESENT EX-PRESIDENT-FOR-LIFE DUVALIER.

GOOD, GOOD. I'LL TELL YOU WHY I CALLED. I'M VERY INTERESTED IN ACQUIRING ONE OF HIS ZOMBIE SLAVES, A MR. LÉGUME.

WHY? SENTIMENTAL REASONS, MOSTLY. MAY WE NEGOTIATE? GREAT. I'M GOING TO PUT ON MY HIGH-POWERED LEGAL COUNSEL, MS. JOANIE "JAWS" CAUCUS.

"JAWS" HERE.

RING! RING! HEY, JAWS! THE ATTORNEY GENERAL ON LINE TWO!

HOW FAR DO YOU WANT TO GO WITH THIS?

AS FAR AS WE HAVE TO. I'M A RICH MAN.

MR. DUPUIS? SINCE THE PURCHASE OF HUMAN BEINGS IS FORBIDDEN OUTSIDE OF PRO SPORTS, MY CLIENT HAS ADVISED ME TO OFFER YOU A "FINDER'S FEE" FOR MR. DUKE'S RETURN.

WHAT DO WE HAVE IN MIND? WELL, THAT'S DIFFICULT TO SAY, MR. DUPUIS. HOW CAN WE MEASURE THE VALUE OF A PERSON? IS IT POSSIBLE TO SET A PRICE FOR A HUMAN LIFE?

$10 MILLION. TAKE IT OR LEAVE IT.

PASS. WE'RE NOT TALKING MOTHER TERESA HERE.

EXCUSE ME, SIR. THERE'S A RUMOR IN THE SLAVE QUARTERS THAT I'M ON THE BLOCK.

THAT'S RIGHT, LÉGUME. A RICH AMERICAN WANTS TO BUY YOU. HE CLAIMS TO BE YOUR NEPHEW.

NEPHEW? YOU MEAN, ZONKER? OH, PLEASE, YOUR MALIGNANCY, NOT HIM! ZONKER'S A MONSTER! CRUELTY INCARNATE! HE'S EVIL ON THE HOOF!

OR IS THAT MY COUSIN ALFREDO? I GET THEM MIXED UP..

IT DOESN'T MATTER. THE DEAL IS AS GOOD AS DONE!

COULDN'T YOU SELL HIM ONE OF THE OTHER GUYS?

SORRY. I ALREADY SENT HIM YOUR BROCHURE.

180

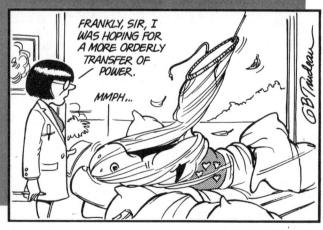

WHAT'S THE WORD FROM THE FRONT, DON?

IT'S CATCHING ON, SIR. CANDIDATES ALL OVER THE COUNTRY ARE ENLISTING IN YOUR WAR AGAINST DRUGS!

UNFORTUNATELY, AS A CAMPAIGN ISSUE, IT SEEMS TO HAVE ONE DRAWBACK: EVERYONE'S ON THE SAME SIDE OF THE ISSUE.

IF ONLY WE COULD FIND A STRAW MAN, SOME HIGH-PROFILE LIBERTARIAN CRAZY OR STUPID ENOUGH TO TAKE A STAND FOR DRUG ABUSE!

I'M NEEDED, HONEY.

SIR! YOU SAID SOMETHING!

...AND THE FOLLOWING PARTS OF THE BILL OF RIGHTS HAVE BEEN SUSPENDED...

SOME WAR ON DRUGS! IT'S SCORCHED EARTH TIME! I'VE GOT TO GET HOME, PRONTO!

THEY'LL LISTEN TO ME! I'M PRESIDENT OF A RESPECTED MEDICAL COLLEGE!

UH...YOU WERE, SIR. LAST WEEK, JUDGE DUPUIS RULED YOU INCOMPETENT.

DUPUIS? THAT TREACHEROUS OLD CROCK OF SLIME! I'VE HAD HIM ON RETAINER FOR TWO YEARS! YOU CAN'T TRUST ANYONE THESE DAYS!

LISTEN, HONEY...

PRESIDENT HONEY.

G.B.Trudeau

HELP ME FIND MY SNEAKERS, HONEY! MY COUNTRY NEEDS ME!

IT'S TOO LATE, SIR. EVERYTHING HAS CHANGED SINCE YOU'VE BEEN GONE.

GONE? I DIDN'T GO ANYWHERE! DID I?

PEOPLE ARE NO LONGER TOLERANT OF DRUG USE. THE COST HAS BEEN TOO HIGH. A LOT OF US NOW THINK IT WAS WRONG TO LOOK THE OTHER WAY!

AFTER NANCY REAGAN'S SPEECH, I REALIZED THAT I'D BEEN REMISS, THAT BY STANDING IDLY DURING YOUR SELF-DESTRUCTIVE BINGES, I'D LET YOU DOWN AS A FRIEND.

YEAH, WELL, DON'T LOSE ANY SLEEP OVER...

I'VE TURNED YOU IN, SIR.

HEY, DID YOU GUYS KNOW THE HOUSE WAS SURROUNDED?

G.B.Trudeau

183

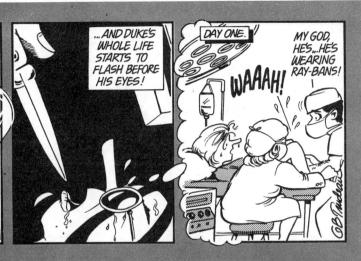

HI. I'M SAL DOONESBURY, AND I'D LIKE TO WELCOME YOU TO THE INSTITUTE FOR IMMACULATE CONTRACEPTION, POPULARLY KNOWN AS WHOOPEE U.!

AS DISTRICT SALES MANAGER TRAINEES, YOU ARE HERE TO LEARN THE WHOOPEE WAY OF LIFE. IT MAY BE THE MOST IMPORTANT COURSE OF INSTRUCTION YOU EVER TAKE!

WHEN YOU SELL DR. WHOOPEE, YOU ARE SELLING HOPE. YOU BECOME PART OF THE SOLUTION. YOU'LL BE SAYING NO TO A MYRIAD OF SOCIAL PROBLEMS!

OF COURSE, YOU'LL ALSO BE WINNING FABULOUS PRIZES!

SAL, HOW MANY POINTS FOR THE CATCHER'S MITT?

BEFORE WE START, LET'S TAKE A LOOK AT THIS MOTIVATIONAL VIDEO MESSAGE FROM DR. WHOOPEE'S FOUNDER AND CHAIRMAN!

CLIK!

YOU KNOW, WHEN I FOUNDED DR. WHOOPEE LAST YEAR, I SWORE MY PRODUCTS WOULD BE THE FINEST AVAILABLE ON THE MARKET! WELL, I DELIVERED ON THAT PLEDGE.

HOW DO YOU KNOW? HOW DO YOU KNOW OUR LINE IS ALL I SAY IT IS? HOW DO YOU KNOW WE USE ONLY THE FINEST MATERIALS CURRENTLY AVAILABLE ANYWHERE IN THE CARIBBEAN BASIN?

TRUST ME.

AN INSPIRATIONAL VIDEO FOR DR. WHOOPEE TRAINEES...

AS FOUNDER OF DR. WHOOPEE, I KEEP AN EAGLE EYE ON OUR PRODUCT FROM START TO FINISH!

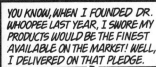

"DR. WHOOPEES ARE STILL MADE BY HAND BY LOCAL HAITIAN CRAFTSPEOPLE USING THE SAME TIME-HONORED METHODS I DEVELOPED BACK IN 1986."

"BY CONTRAST, OUR DISTRIBUTION IS STATE-OF-THE-ART. ORDERS ARE RELAYED BY SATELLITE AND PROCESSED BY COMPUTER!"

MEANWHILE, IN RESEARCH AND DEVELOPMENT...

EUREKA! PLAID!

DOONESBURY! *WHY THE HELL HAVEN'T YOU MOVED THAT LAST CONSIGNMENT OF DR. WHOOPEES?*

SORRY, SIR...

...BUT TWO OF MY TOP GUYS TOOK OFF FOR THE HARMONIC CONVERGENCE.

WHAT?

LISTEN, SAL, NO MORE HIPPIE HOLIDAYS! IF YOUR PEOPLE WANT TO CAVORT WITH SPOOKS, LET THEM DO IT ON THEIR **OWN** TIME! **GOT** IT?

EXCUSE ME, SIR, THERE'S A WILLIAM CASEY HERE TO SEE YOU.

UH...LET ME GET BACK TO YOU, SAL...

BILL...BILL CASEY... MY GOD, IT **IS** YOU!

LONG TIME, DUKE.

THIS IS ABSOLUTELY INCREDIBLE...

I MEAN, YOUR BEING HERE IN HAITI! AND LOOKING SO **WELL!** I MEAN, CONSIDERING THAT, YOU KNOW... I MEAN, THIS IS HARD TO... / TO...

LET'S CUT THE CRAP, BILL. YOU'RE DEAD.

A LEADING THEORY, IT'S TRUE.

HOW...HOW'D YOU PULL IT OFF, BILL? THE WHOLE WORLD THINKS YOU'RE DEAD!

I'M A SPOOK, DUKE. DECEIT HAS BEEN MY LIFE.

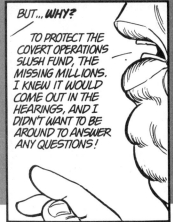

BUT...**WHY?**

TO PROTECT THE COVERT OPERATIONS SLUSH FUND, THE MISSING MILLIONS. I KNEW IT WOULD COME OUT IN THE HEARINGS, AND I DIDN'T WANT TO BE AROUND TO ANSWER ANY QUESTIONS!

IT'S TOO BRILLIANT A PLAN TO GIVE UP, DUKE. SINCE THE MONEY ISN'T APPROPRIATED, THE PRESIDENT WOULD HAVE A COMPLETELY DISCRETIONARY, ALBEIT ILLEGAL, COVERT CAPABILITY!

SO WHERE DO **I** FIT IN?

AS I SAY, IT'S ILLEGAL.

THE POSSIBILITIES ARE FANTASTIC, DUKE! WE COULD FUND THE CONTRAS, BUY THE AFGHANS NUKES, TERMINATE PANAMA'S PRESIDENT!

EXCUSE ME A MINUTE, WILL YOU, BILL?

HONEY!

YES, SIR?

AM I ON ANYTHING RIGHT NOW?

LET ME CHECK YOUR BOOK, SIR...

DUKE, LET ME COME RIGHT TO THE POINT...

I'M ALL EARS, BILL!

THIS COVERT ACTION SLUSH FUND IS THE GREATEST INNOVATION IN U.S. INTELLIGENCE IN A GENERATION. I'M PROUD OF IT. I DON'T WANT TO SEE IT DIE WITH ME!

NOR I, BILL.

I NEED YOUR HELP, DUKE. I NEED SOMEONE WHO CAN LEAD THE ILLEGAL COVERT OPERATIONS OF THIS COUNTRY INTO THE TWENTY-FIRST CENTURY!

GEE, I DUNNO, BILL. I GOT A LOT ON MY PLATE AND...

CLIK!

FOR AN OBSCENE FEE, OF COURSE.

OBSCENE? HOW OBSCENE? HAITI HAS DIFFERENT COMMUNITY STANDARDS.

OBVIOUSLY, DUKE, I CAN'T USE COMPANY PERSONNEL ANYMORE. THAT'S WHY I NEED YOU TO ASSEMBLE A COVERT ACTION TEAM!

HERE'S THE COMPLETE FINANCIAL RECORD. TAKE A LOOK, SO YOU KNOW WHAT YOU'VE GOT TO WORK WITH. I'LL GIVE YOU THE ACCOUNT NUMBER WHEN YOU'RE READY TO GO!

THERE'S NO TIME TO WASTE, DUKE. I'M NOT A WELL MAN. IN FACT...>COUGH!< I MAY NOT...

TOP SECRET

>COUGH!<
>COUGH!<
HACK!
HACK!

CRASH!!

JEEZ, BILL, THIS IS ONE HELLUVA HAND-OFF.

190

I'M A MAN OF RESPECT. I EXPECT TO BE TREATED LIKE ONE. YOU FOLLOW ME?

WHEN I SPOT SOMEONE $230,000, I EXPECT TO SEE IT AGAIN. I'M A BUSINESSMAN. IF I GET STIFFED, I LOSE FACE. AND THAT'S BAD FOR BUSINESS.

HEY, YOU WANT A NEW SUIT? YOU WANT I SHOULD HAVE YOU MEASURED FOR A SUIT, TOO?

UH... SURE. WOOL?

CONCRETE. YOU'RE IN A WORLD OF TROUBLE, DOG MEAT.

LOOK, I WAS **GOING** TO PAY YOU BACK! I **SWEAR** IT! BUT WHAT COULD I DO? WHO KNEW MY MOTHER WOULD NEED SURGERY?

PSST, SIR! DON'T YOU THINK YOU SHOULD LEVEL WITH THIS GUY? HE COULD BE A FEDERAL AGENT!

SHUT UP, HONEY. HE'S JOHN GOTTI, HEAD OF THE GAMBINO FAMILY!

OH.

CARRY ON, SIR.

YOU'VE GOT A MOTHER, RIGHT, BIG GUY? RIGHT?

LEMME TELL YOU SOMETHING, DUKE. I'M AN ACQUITTED MAN. I LIKE THE ACQUITTED LIFE VERY MUCH. I'M THE ROSE OF HOWARD BEACH!

SO I GOTTA BE CAREFUL, UNDERSTAND? THAT'S WHY I'M GONNA LET YOU GUESS WHAT I WANT FROM YOU, AND WHAT'LL HAPPEN TO YOU IF I DON'T GET IT.

YOU WANT 10% OF MY BUSINESS OR I GET MY HANDS BROKEN?

GUESS AGAIN.

YOU GET 90% OR I GET STUFFED INTO A CAR COMPACTER?

IS THAT A **GUESS?** HOW COME YOUSE GUYS DON'T GUESS THAT GOOD?

HEY, C'MON, BOSS, HE GOT LUCKY!

195
195

LOOK AT THE QUALITY! CHAMOIS LEATHER WALLS! BIRD'S EYE MAPLE TRIM! HAND-CARVED ONYX BATHROOMS! WE'RE TALKING **QUALITY**! A LEVEL OF QUALITY THAT'S HARD TO EXPLAIN!

TRUMP PRINCESS

LOOK HERE, **MORE** QUALITY...

EXCUSE ME, SIR. BY "QUALITY", YOU MEAN IT **COSTS** AN OBSCENE AMOUNT, RIGHT?

UH... RIGHT.

THERE ARE OTHER DEFINITIONS?

NONE THAT MATTER. I WAS JUST CHECKING.

LOOK AT THE PERFORMANCE QUALITY OF THIS BOAT! 17.5 KNOTS CRUISING SPEED! 8,500 MILES WITHOUT REFUELING! YOU CAN'T JUST **BUY** THIS KIND OF QUALITY, YOU HAVE TO **WILL** IT!

DO YOU THINK YOU CAN HANDLE HER, CAPTAIN?

NO PROBLEM, MR. TRUMP!

OKAY, SEE THAT LITTLE OUTBOARD OVER THERE?

WITH THE KIDS? YEAH, I SEE IT.

SWAMP IT.

PIECE OF CAKE.

ON THE BOARDWALK.

MAGNIFICENT, ISN'T SHE?

YEAH. IF YOU'RE A LITTLE BOY INTO GIGANTIC TOYS.

TAKES YOUR BREATH AWAY, DOESN'T IT?

I'LL SAY. YOU DON'T OFTEN SEE VULGARITY ON THAT SCALE.

QUITE A SIGHT, EH?

DO YOU REALIZE TRUMP COULD HAVE BUILT 800 UNITS OF LOW-INCOME HOUSING WITH WHAT HE PAID FOR THAT THING?

LATER...

WELL?

AS YOU SUSPECTED, BIG GUY! THEY LOVE YA!

...AND WHILE EVERYONE ELSE WAS WAITING FOR THE PRICE TO GO DOWN, I STEPPED IN WITH $30 MILLION CASH AND SNAPPED UP A BOAT WHOSE REPLACEMENT VALUE IS $180 MILLION!

IT WAS A NEGOTIATING TRIUMPH! THE "TRUMP PRINCESS" IS A FLOATING TRIBUTE TO THE ART OF MAKING A DEAL!

HEE, HEE!

WHAT'S SO FUNNY, CAPTAIN?

NOTHING'S FUNNY, SIR. I JUST LOVE THAT YOU CALL DEALMAKING AN "ART."

CLASSY, HUH? IT WAS MY WIFE'S IDEA.

IT REALLY PUTS PAINTING AND LITERATURE IN THEIR PLACE.

I GUESS COMING DOWN HERE WAS A GOOD IDEA, MR. TRUMP! LOOK AT THE RECEPTION YOU'RE GETTING!

WELL, OF COURSE, CAPTAIN! WHETHER IN ATLANTIC CITY OR NEW ORLEANS, THERE WILL ALWAYS BE AN AUDIENCE FOR QUALITY!

THESE ARE MY PEOPLE, CAPTAIN, THE STRIVERS, THE WANNA-BES, THE LITTLE PEOPLE WITH BIG DREAMS!

YOO-HOO! DONALD! OVER HERE!

WARNING!

YOU SEEN THE VICE PRESIDENT, SENATOR?

NO, HE DIDN'T MAKE IT. FROM WHAT I HEAR, HIS HANDLERS ARE KEEPING HIM UNDER WRAPS UNTIL TOMORROW.

THEY FIGURE REAGAN'S RECEPTION IN THE BOWL TONIGHT COULD PROVE EMBARRASSING.

EMBARRASSING? THAT'S PUTTING IT MILDLY.

FOUR MORE YEARS! FOUR MORE YEARS!

SIGH...

IS THE BUSHMAN ON YET?

IN A MOMENT...

HIS SON IS INTRODUCING HIM NOW.

HIS SON MADE A VIDEO?

IT'S NOT A VIDEO. IT'S A SLIDE SHOW.

SLIDE SHOW?

NEXT, PLEASE. OKAY, THIS IS MY DAD'S 25-YEAR-OLD GOLF CART...

...AND SO GEORGE BUSH HAS SPELLED OUT WHAT HE CALLS "THE VISION THING."

IT IS, LARGELY, A VISION OF MORE OF THE SAME, ONLY WITH FEWER PEOPLE GOING TO JAIL. STILL NO WORD ON WHO'S PAYING FOR IT.

AND NOW, AT THE MOMENT OF GEORGE BUSH'S GREATEST POLITICAL TRIUMPH, HE IS JOINED AT THE PODIUM BY THE ENTIRE BUSH CLAN!

NEAT SPEECH, DAD!

I KICKED **TAIL!** I KICKED **TAIL!**

WASN'T THAT UNCLE SKIPPY?

THE RETURN VOYAGE OF THE "TRUMP PRINCESS" FROM NEW ORLEANS WAS UNEVENTFUL...

MORE CAVIAR TOPSIDES!

AYE, AYE, SIR!

...UNTIL THE FATEFUL MORNING WHEN THE PURSER SPOTTED A FAMILIAR FIGURE LEANING AGAINST THE RADIO MAST.

MY GOD! IT **CAN'T** BE!

LATER, THE NIGHT MAID CONFIRMED THE SIGHTING.

IT'S...YOU!

THE CAPTAIN WAS DULY NOTIFIED.

SIR? ELVIS IS ON BOARD.

OH, YEAH? BOOK HIM FOR TONIGHT.

IT'S TRUE, SIR. ELVIS IS ON BOARD.

YOU DON'T SAY...

HOW'D HE GET ON BOARD?

WE DON'T KNOW, SIR. HE APPEARS TO BE A STOW-AWAY!

WHERE'S HE NOW?

HE'S ON THE POOL DECK. HITTING ON THE TOWEL GIRL.

HEY, BABY! EVER HEAR OF THE KING?

PLEASE.

GOOD TO MEET YA, CAPTAIN...

I KNEW YOU WERE ALIVE, KING. I NEVER GAVE UP HOPE.

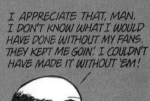

I APPRECIATE THAT, MAN. I DON'T KNOW WHAT I WOULD HAVE DONE WITHOUT MY FANS. THEY KEPT ME GOIN'! I COULDN'T HAVE MADE IT WITHOUT 'EM!

SO WHERE **HAVE** YOU BEEN ALL THESE YEARS, KING?

WELL, BELIEVE IT OR NOT, THEM TABLOID PAPERS ACTU-ALLY GOT IT RIGHT!

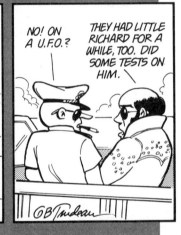

NO! ON A U.F.O.?

THEY HAD LITTLE RICHARD FOR A WHILE, TOO. DID SOME TESTS ON HIM.

TRUMP, NOTIFIED OF ELVIS' PRE-SENCE ON HIS YACHT, CHOPPERS TO THE "TRUMP PRINCESS" AT ONCE.

I DON'T CARE WHAT IT COSTS! I WANT ELVIS TO PLAY MY ATLANTIC CITY CASINOS!

I HEAR YOU, MR. T!

PUT HIM IN THE DIAMOND SUITE! AND TAKE CARE OF HIM! WHAT ELVIS WANTS, ELVIS **GETS**!

I'M WAY AHEAD OF YOU, SIR.

AMPHETAMINES, SIR! COMPLI-MENTS OF THE CAPTAIN!

Y'ALL ARE GREAT, MAN.

THANK YOU VERY MUCH, LADIES AND GENTLEMEN. IT'S GOOD TO BE BACK.

THE PEOPLE HERE AT TRUMP PLAZA TOLD ME Y'ALL WANTED TO HEAR MY OLD HITS, SONGS LIKE "HEARTBREAK HOTEL" AND "DON'T BE CRUEL..."

BUT I TOLD 'EM, I GOTTA BE ME. TONIGHT I WANNA PLAY SOMETHIN' DIFFERENT FOR Y'ALL. LADIES AND GENTLEMEN, THE MUSIC OF MY GOOD FRIEND, MR. JOHN DENVER!

DAMN... DID YOU CALL THE RIOT POLICE?

THEY'RE ON ALERT.

ROCKY MOUNTAIN HIIIGH!

IT'S AN OUTRAGE! FIRST THE GUY CHARGED $1500 A TICKET FOR A 90-SECOND FIGHT! NOW HE'S RIPPED OFF $2500 A HEAD TO SEE SOME BLIMPO ELVIS IMPOSTER SING "ROCKY MOUNTAIN HIGH"!

I'M ROLAND HEDLEY. IT'S A BAD NIGHT FOR CASINO OPERATOR DON TRUMP AS HIS MUCH BALLY-HOOED RETURN OF ELVIS HAS ERUPTED INTO UGLY MAYHEM.

ANOTHER CLEAR LOSER HERE TONIGHT: GEORGE BUSH, WHOSE CAMPAIGN APPEARANCE HAS BEEN COMPLETELY UPSTAGED BY THE VIOLENT REACTION TO THE ABORTED CONCERT.

...AND IF I'M ELECTED, I DARN SURE WON'T BURN THE FLAG!

KILL TRUMP! KILL TRUMP!

THE BOSS SUMMONS DUKE FOR THEIR WEEKLY CONFAB.

...AND MY WIFE WILL BOARD TODAY. SEND A LITTER.

CHECK.

OH, ONE MORE THING. I'VE HIRED A NEW SOCIAL DI-RECTOR.

SOCIAL DIRECTOR?

YEAH. I'D LIKE YOU TO MEET HER. MARILYN, SEND IN MISS HUAN.

HOLD IT...

FATE! THERE'S NO OTHER WORD FOR IT, SIR!

CAN YOU BELIEVE IT, SIR? THE WINDS OF DESTINY HAVE TOSSED US TOGETHER AGAIN!

ISN'T IT GREAT, SIR? A FRESH START! A CHANCE TO SHIP OUT AND SHAPE UP TOGETHER! WHO **SAYS** THERE ARE NO SECOND ACTS IN AMERICA? SIR? HELLO?

CAPTAIN, YOU DON'T SEEM TOO THRILLED TO SEE THIS YOUNG WOMAN...

SHE'S JUST A FLASHBACK, SIR. SHE'LL GO AWAY.

NO, SIR, IT'S REALLY ME! TOUCH ME! DISCREETLY, OF COURSE.

SO MUCH HAS HAPPENED SINCE WE SAW EACH OTHER LAST, SIR...

I WAS AFRAID OF THAT.

FIRST, WE HAD A LABOR DISPUTE AT DR. WHOOPEE, AND A DISGRUNTLED FORMER EMPLOYEE ATTACKED ME IN THE EXECUTIVE WASHROOM WITH A SPATULA...

AFTER THAT, I HAD A TORRID PLATONIC RELATIONSHIP WITH A CAPO FROM THE GAMBINO FAMILY, WHICH ENDED WHEN I TOLD HIM I WANTED HIS BABY. THEN I HAD A SELF-DESTRUCTIVE CRUSH ON...

HEY! DID I ASK? DID I **ASK?**

NO, SIR. AND FRANKLY, I'M A LITTLE HURT.

...AND THEN A FRIEND OF A FRIEND INTRODUCED ME TO MRS. TRUMP'S PERSONNEL DIRECTOR!

SO EVERYTHING TURNED OUT GREAT, ALTHOUGH FOR A WHILE THERE THINGS LOOKED PRETTY GRIM...

IT TOOK ME A LONG TIME TO GET OVER BEING ATTACKED BY THAT MADMAN WITH A SPATULA. THE POLICE NEVER IDENTIFIED HIM.

IT WAS ME.

WELL, I THOUGHT SO, BUT I COULDN'T FIND YOU IN THE MUG BOOK.

DAY 20.

IT'S A MESS DOWN THERE, SIR. WE'RE BASICALLY BUILDING ALL OF PANAMA'S GOVERNING INSTITUTIONS FROM SCRATCH!

WHAT WE URGENTLY NEED IS A CIVILIAN ADMINISTRATOR, SOMEONE ON THE GROUND WHO CAN DIRECT THE RECONSTRUCTION OF THE COUNTRY!

GOT ANYONE IN MIND?

YES, SIR. A RETIRED FOREIGN SERVICE OFFICER WITH GOOD COLONIAL EXPERIENCE. HE'LL DO IT IF WE CAN SETTLE ON A TITLE.

OKAY, HOW ABOUT "MAXIMUM PROCONSUL"?

DONE! FAX MY CONTRACT TO SOUTHERN COMMAND!

SORRY, DUKE, I CAN'T SPARE YOU. I'M GONNA HOLD YOU TO YOUR CONTRACT!

BUT MR. T, THIS APPOINTMENT TO PANAMA IS A **MAJOR** OPPORTUNITY...

PANAMA CITY IS THE NEXT HAVANA, THE NEXT SAIGON! IT'S WIDE OPEN, AND AS PROCONSUL, **I'LL** BE MAKING THE DECISIONS ON DEVELOPMENT—HOUSING, HOTELS, CASINOS, THE **WORKS!**

DON'T BE A STRANGER.

AYE, AYE, SIR!

SIR, MAY I BE THE FIRST TO CONGRATULATE YOU ON YOUR APPOINTMENT TO MAXIMUM PROCONSUL OF PANAMA. I ONLY WISH I COULD JOIN YOU!

UNFORTUNATELY, SINCE OUR DIVORCE, I'VE DEVELOPED ROOTS AND COMMITMENTS RIGHT HERE IN NEW JERSEY. I HAVE A NICE HOME THAT I'VE JUST DECORATED...

...AND I HAVE TWO CATS AND FOUR PLANTS THAT NEED ME. I ALSO HAVE A JOB I LOVE, FOR WHICH I AM BOTH APPRECIATED AND WELL-COMPENSATED!

WHAT A SHAME. I NEED SOMEONE TO TASTE MY FOOD.

I'LL GO PACK.

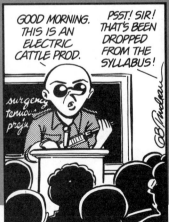

PROCONSUL DUKE TALKS TO PANAMA'S NEW "PUBLIC FORCE."

THE IMPORTANT THING FOR YOU TO REMEMBER IS THAT IN THE NEW PANAMA, YOU GOTTA GO BY THE BOOK— OUR BOOK!

NOW, I DON'T LIKE IT ANY MORE THAN YOU, BUT THAT'S THE DOWN SIDE OF A REAL DEMOCRACY— FOR SOME REASON, CRIMINALS HAVE RIGHTS!

WHAT KIND OF RIGHTS, SEÑOR PROCONSUL?

UM...WELL, FOR STARTERS, YOU CAN'T DO ANY-THING CRUEL OR UNU-SUAL.

BUT YOUR SOLDIERS MADE NORI-EGA LISTEN TO RAP MUSIC FOR A WEEK!

THAT WAS STILL PART OF THE INVASION. DOESN'T COUNT.

SEÑOR, WILL WE GET TO WEAR ITALIAN SPORTS JACKETS?

MEN, AS PANAMA'S NEW PEACE OFFICERS, IT'LL BE UP TO YOU TO MAKE THIS A COUNTRY WE CAN ALL BE PROUD OF!

PANAMA'S BEING GIVEN ONE MORE CHANCE TO EMULATE THE AMERI-CAN MODEL OF DEMOCRACY. YOU HAVE A FREELY ELECTED PRESI-DENT, YOU HAVE A CONSTITU-TION, YOU HAVE FOUNDING FATHERS...

WHAT FOUNDING FATHERS?

THE 82ND AIRBORNE. REVERE THEM.

HOW ABOUT A DECLARA-TION OF INDEPEN-DENCE?

DON'T GET CUTE. CLASS DISMISSED.

LISTEN, COLONEL, AFTER WE CLEAR OUT OF HERE, YOU CAN GO BACK TO YOUR OWN WAY OF KEEPING ORDER! BUT UNTIL THEN, I'VE GOT A DEMOCRACY TO RUN!

YOU'VE GOT TO FIND A FEW MEN FOR THE PUBLIC FORCE WHO WEREN'T IN THE P.D.F.! EVERYONE THINKS ALL WE'VE DONE IS CHANGE THE SHOULDER PATCHES!

SI, SEÑOR PROCONSUL, BUT THE PEOPLE RESPECT MY MEN!

ARE YOU KIDDING? THEY LOATHE THEM! 92% OF THE PANAMANIAN PEO-PLE SUPPORT THE INVASION!

IF YOU SAY SO, SEÑOR. SHOULD WE DETAIN THE OTHER 8%?

YOU STILL DON'T GET IT, DO YOU?

THE PROCONSUL GETS A CALL.

MR. DUKE? THIS IS THE PRESIDENT! HOW'S DANNY MAKING OUT?

WELL, HE'S MAKIN' A HELLUVA IMPRESSION, SIR!

I WAS AFRAID OF THAT. WHAT'S HE DOING NOW?

INSPECTING THE INVASION FORCE, SIR. HE'S WORRIED ABOUT THEIR UNIFORMS.

THEIR UNIFORMS? WHAT'S WRONG WITH THEM?

THEY'RE JUNGLE-STYLE CAMOUFLAGE, SIR. THE VICE PRESIDENT THINKS THEY'RE INAPPROPRIATE FOR URBAN COMBAT.

CAN WE GET UNIFORMS WITH LITTLE BUILDINGS ON THEM?

WE'LL TRY, SIR!

SO HOW ARE THE TROOPS, MR. VICE PRESIDENT?

GOOD! THEY LOOKED TAN, RESTED, NOT AT ALL LIKE THEY'D BEEN IN AN INVASION!

THE ONLY PROBLEM IS THEY'RE STILL HERE. THE WHOLE REASON I CAME DOWN HERE WAS TO REASSURE OUR FRIENDS THAT THIS WAS A SHORT-TERM, ONE-TIME INTERVENTION!

IT'S NOT EASY CARRYING A MESSAGE LIKE THAT ALL OVER LATIN AMERICA—TO COUNTRIES LIKE... LIKE... WHAT'S THAT ONE WITH THE BEACHES?

WHATEVER.

RIGHT. ESPECIALLY IF YOU DON'T SPEAK A **WORD** OF LATIN!

PRESIDENT VARGAS? PRO-CONSUL DUKE HERE! LISTEN, I GOT DAN QUAYLE HERE SITTING IN MY OFFICE...

HE'S MADE A HECK OF AN EFFORT TO GET DOWN HERE. AND I THINK MORE OF YOU GUYS SHOULD BE HEARING HIM OUT...

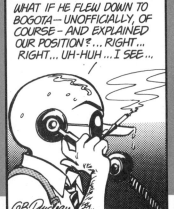
WHAT IF HE FLEW DOWN TO BOGOTA—UNOFFICIALLY, OF COURSE—AND EXPLAINED OUR POSITION?... RIGHT... RIGHT... UH-HUH... I SEE...

HE'S AFRAID YOU'LL BE DRAGGED FROM YOUR LIMO AND BEATEN WITH PIPES.

DAMN... OKAY, LET'S TRY THE PRESIDENT OF PUERTO RICO!

LOOK, PRESIDENT ARIAS, I APPRECIATE YOUR POSITION, BUT COME ON, THE INVASION WASN'T DANNY QUAYLE'S CALL! **NOTHING** IS! WHY TAKE IT OUT ON HIM?

BECAUSE THE NATIONS OF THIS REGION HAVE HAD ENOUGH, MR. PROCONSUL.

ENOUGH? ENOUGH OF WHAT?

IN 1901, THE U.S. SENT TROOPS TO COLOMBIA; IN 1902, TO PANAMA; IN 1903, HONDURAS, DOMINICAN REPUBLIC AND PANAMA; IN 1904, DOMINICAN REPUBLIC AND PANAMA; 1906, CUBA; 1907, HONDURAS; 1910, NICARAGUA; 1911, HONDURAS; 1912...

WELL? WELL?

BAD LUCK. HE'S A HISTORY NUT.

LOOK, PRESIDENT GARCIA PEREZ, YOU'VE GOT TO TAKE THE LONG VIEW HERE! SOONER OR LATER, BUSH IS GONNA SEND QUAYLE TO PERU WHETHER YOU LIKE IT OR NOT!

WHY NOT JUST GET IT OVER WITH? WHAT?...UH-HUH...RIGHT... HOW WOULD THAT WORK? UH-HUH... OKAY, LET ME FLY IT BY HIM.

HE SAYS YOU CAN COME IF YOU SLIP ACROSS THE BOLIVIAN BORDER, DON A DISGUISE AND RIDE BY BURRO 250 MILES TO A REMOTE MONASTERY OUTSIDE OF CUZCO, WHERE YOU WOULD MEET WITH A RANKING GOVERNMENT OFFICIAL.

A **RANKING** OFFICIAL? WOW...

ALERT THE MONKS.

WERE YOU ABLE TO OPEN ANY DOORS FOR THE VEEP, SIR?

YEAH, POSSIBLY PERU.

GARCIA PEREZ SAYS HE CAN COME AS LONG AS HE'S WILLING TO PUT ON A DISGUISE AND RIDE A DONKEY THROUGH THE ANDES FOR A SECRET MEET AT A MONASTERY.

DANNY'S GAME, BUT HE'S STILL GOTTA RUN IT BY THE BIG GUY.

DANNY, COME HOME.

AW, SIR! I ALREADY GOT MY DISGUISE!

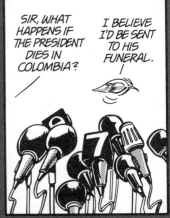

218

HOW WE MAKING OUT, SIR?

LIKE GANG-BUSTERS, HONEY! DOUBLING THE COVER CHARGE DIDN'T HURT A BIT!

I SEE YOU HIRED A NEW BAR-TENDER...

HAD TO. WE'RE DOING SERIOUS VOLUME NOW. WE CAN'T GET CAUGHT SHORT-HANDED.

BESIDES, THE GUY'S A REAL PRO. HE KNOWS HIS INVENTORY, AND HE KNOWS HOW TO LISTEN.

...,AND, OF COURSE, IN A TANK, YOU CAN'T SMOKE AT ALL!

YOU POOR KID!

HONEY, LET'S ADMIT IT, WE'RE ON A ROLL — BIG TIME! AND IT AIN'T GONNA QUIT SOON!

WE GOT A BUILT-IN CLIENTELE FOR YEARS TO COME — THE ENGINEERS, THE CONTRACTORS, THE WEAPONS SALESMEN, THE DIPLOMATS, THE PRESS!

HELL, THE CITY'S SWARMING WITH RANK, SWEATY OPPORTUNISTS HERE ONLY TO FEED OFF THE DETRITUS OF THIS COUNTRY'S TRAGEDY!

SORT OF LIKE US.

EXACTAMENTO! DID YOU PAY OFF THE MILITIA THIS WEEK?

SO HOW'S THE TILL LOOK TONIGHT, HONEY?

EXCEL-LENT, SIR.

THE BOYS FROM THE HOUSTON FIRE-FIGHTING COMPANIES GOT PAID TODAY. THEY'RE SPENDING MONEY LIKE THEY'VE NEVER EVEN HEARD OF ALIMONY BEFORE!

I MUST SAY, THEY LOOK QUITE GLAMOROUS IN THEIR OIL-SOAKED JUMPSUITS. I JUST WISH THEY WOULDN'T START SO MANY FIGHTS...

HEY, JERK-FACE! WATCH THE SPARKS, OKAY?

OH... SORRY.

GOOD EVENING, FOLKS! I'D LIKE TO WELCOME YOU TO CLUB SCUD, ESPECIALLY THE OIL WELL CAPPERS FROM RED ADAIR AND THE OTHER TEXAN OUTFITS!

I THINK YOU'LL FIND OUR ESTABLISHMENT AN OASIS OF GOOD CHEER AND REFRESHMENT IN THE OTHERWISE DRY AND BLASTED LANDSCAPE THAT IS POST-WAR KUWAIT!

WHETHER IT'S THE IMPECCABLY MIXED COCKTAILS OR THE CRISPLY STARCHED TABLECLOTHS, WE HAVE SPARED NO EFFORT IN MAKING YOUR CLUB A PLACE OF DISTINCTION AND CLASS!

NOW THEN, SOMEONE ASKED ME ABOUT OUR MISS DESERT STORM WET T-SHIRT CONTEST...

THAT WAS ME. I WAS JUST CURIOUS.

SORRY THE BOYS AIN'T SCRUBBED TODAY. OUR WATER LINE WENT DOWN...

FINE WITH ME, SIR. I LIKE THE MANLY SCENT OF SWEET CRUDE!

WELL, YOU KINDA HAVE TO IF YOU'RE GONNA HANG WITH WELL-KILLERS! WE DO GET DOUSED WITH JUICE! SOMETIMES OUR OWN WIVES CAN'T TELL US APART. HEE, HEE!

HEE...

PROBABLY WHY I'M ON MY FIFTH MARRIAGE.

I WAS GOING TO SAY.

MAN... WHAT A DAY! RAN OVER ANOTHER LAWN DART!

WHAT'S A LAWN DART, SIR? SOUNDS DANGEROUS.

UNEXPLODED CLUSTER BOMB. BLEW A TREAD CLEAN OFF MY BULLDOZER!

WOW... YOU KNOW, YOU GUYS ARE THE HEROES NOW!

UH-HUH... HEY, LISTEN, KID, YOU WANT A FRIENDLY PIECE OF ADVICE?

FROM YOU, SIR? I'D BE HONORED!

GET A HAIRCUT. YOU LOOK LIKE A GIRL.

THANK YOU, SIR.

KUWAIT HIGH SCHOOL 1991 YEARBOOK

$\mathcal{W}$hat a year it's been for the seniors! First, classes were suspended for the fall and winter. Most of us left for Cairo or Gstaad. Then, liberation! What a hoot! As Prince Tariq "Disco" Al-Amiri put it, "Saddam Hussein can eat my shorts!" Even with no classes, five guys got into Princeton and three into UCLA, so the year wasn't a total loss. Also, there was the senior prom -- talk about a blast! Thanks to Sheik al-Sabah for letting us use his townhouse in London, and to the whole class for showing so much spirit. Go, Scorpions!

YOUSSEF AL-MIAZ
"Al" "The Man"
Class President... Slept through the invasion... Treasurer for neighborhood resistance cell... "Grow up!"...Quote: "Down with the dens of treason and shame, as mentioned in our previous communique."

HAMED AL-MESBAH
"Ham" "Pee-Wee"
Vice President... illegal editorial... weenie reforms ... boycotted Emir's party... working at McDonald's... "sweet spot" on a baseball... Ambition: "to move Kuwait into the 15th century."

ABDEL AL-SABAH
"Prince" "Your Majesty"
Class Treasurer... "I'm outa here!"... Christmas in Aspen... Waterbombing his bodyguard... CNN freak... Bootsie in Bahrain... Trying to grow a mustache... Gold sneaker eyelets... Polo I, II.

AHMAD SALMAN
"Stinky" "Traitor"
Class Secretary... P.L.O. donation boxes... Only guy in school who could fix the air conditioning... "Go, Intifada!"... Soccer I, II... Uncle Hussein... Missing for two months.